The Foot and Shoeing

by

Major C. DAVENPORT

The Pony Club
National Equestrian Centre
Kenilworth, Warwickshire, CV8 2LR

Published in 1977 by
BARRON'S
Woodbury, New York

First Edition 1958

Published in 1977 by
Barron's Educational Series, Inc.
113 Crossways Park Drive
Woodbury, New York 11797

Library of Congress Catalog Card No. 76-55015

Library of Congress Cataloging in Publication Data
Davenport, Colin.
  The foot and shoeing.
   1. Horseshoeing—Addresses, essays, lectures.
I. Title.
SF907.D4   682'.1   76-55015
ISBN 0-8120-0758-1

International Standard Book No. 0-8120-0758-1

Contents

INTRODUCTION and PICTURE No. 1

My talk to you today is the important one of shoeing. It is important because of its intimate connection with the working capabilities of your pony and the length of his useful life.

Many people feel that shoeing is a subject best left to the blacksmith because it is difficult to do and difficult to understand. To shoe a horse certainly is difficult and requires years of practice and experience. To understand about shoeing can be quite simple, and every good equestrian should know something about it if he or she has the interest of the pony at heart. I will try to make my subject both simple and interesting.

To put shoes on a pony's feet is at the best an unnatural act. So is putting a saddle on a pony's back. Nature never intended ponies to wear shoes nor to carry saddles. Our ability to do either without injury to the pony requires that we shall have some understanding of the structures we are dealing with and the kind of damage that will result from ignorance. So let us see first of all something of the structure and function of the pony's foot, and nature's intention in relation to both. Please note that in instances where the pronouns *he* and *him* appear, they have been used to avoid awkward prose. It should be understood that these references apply to both men and women.

Peter Biegel made this drawing for you at the forge in Wiltshire which was the scene of Longfellow's poem.

Part One

THE STRUCTURE OF THE FOOT

For practical purposes a foot consists of three parts: the wall, the sole and the frog. All of these are composed of nonsensitive horn, which explains why shoeing nails can be driven through the wall without causing the pony pain.

The Wall

The wall of the foot is the part you see when the foot is on the ground. Here is the first picture showing this.

PICTURE No. 2

The wall, as you know, extends right round the foot so affording it protection on all sides. It is correct to speak of the *toe* of the foot, the *quarters* and the *heels*.

PICTURE No. 3

Around the top is the *coronary band* from which the wall grows. The hoof is constantly growing from

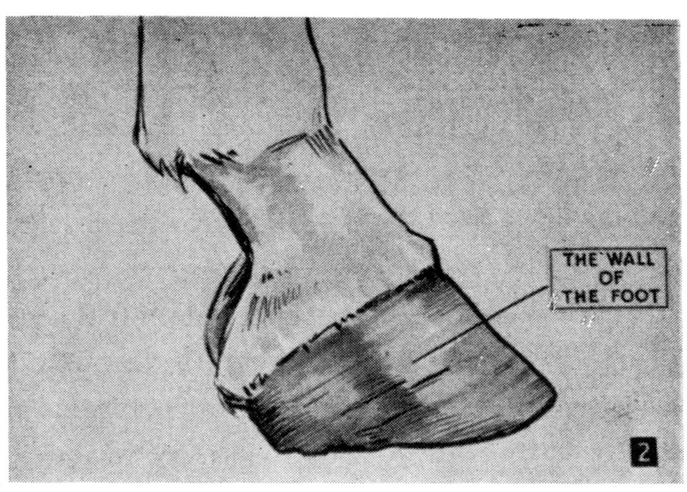

THE WALL
OF
THE FOOT
2

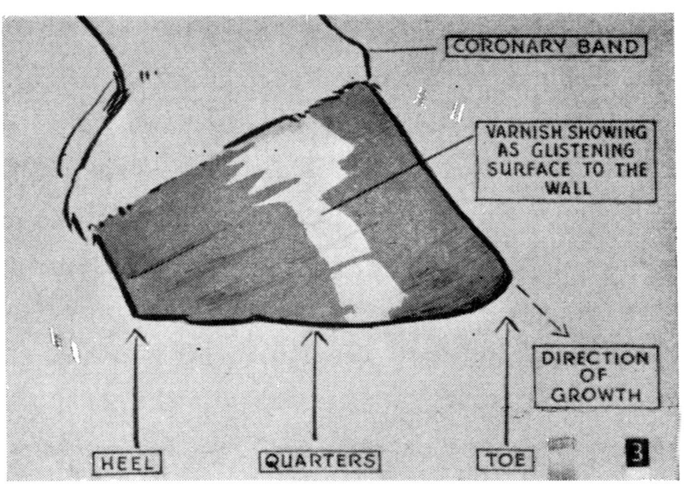

CORONARY BAND
VARNISH SHOWING
AS GLISTENING
SURFACE TO THE
WALL
DIRECTION
OF
GROWTH
HEEL
QUARTERS
TOE
3

above downwards just like your fingernail of which indeed it is the counterpart. Thus wearing away of the wall at the bottom, occasioned by contact with the ground, is made good by new horn constantly growing down from the top.

There is one feature of the wall to which it is necessary to draw special attention. Nature has given the wall a protective coat or varnish which covers it completely, the object of which is to prevent evaporation of moisture from the horn beneath. This coat is difficult to see but may be recognised as the glistening surface to the wall or to your fingernail. All healthy horn contains some small degree of moisture but if this dries away then the horn becomes hard and brittle. This coat is provided to prevent this happening. Any interference with this coat, as for example in abuse of the rasp on the wall in shoeing, results in the removal of the coat with consequent drying up of the horn beneath. This is one of the most fruitful causes of those brittle and broken feet that are all too often seen. It will be a real help to us all if we realise that this coating does exist, why it has been provided and how important it is that it should not be rasped away.

Before leaving the wall let us lift the foot and look at it from the underside.

PICTURE No. 4

Here you see the wall at ground level. You will note that where the wall reaches the heels it is reflected forward to form what are called the *bars* of the foot. These provide support for the frog and act as a buttress on each side on which the frog can press. These bars ought not to be interfered with in shoeing. Cutting away of the bars by the blacksmith is called 'opening up the foot' and is a bad practice and one, though common years ago, is rare today.

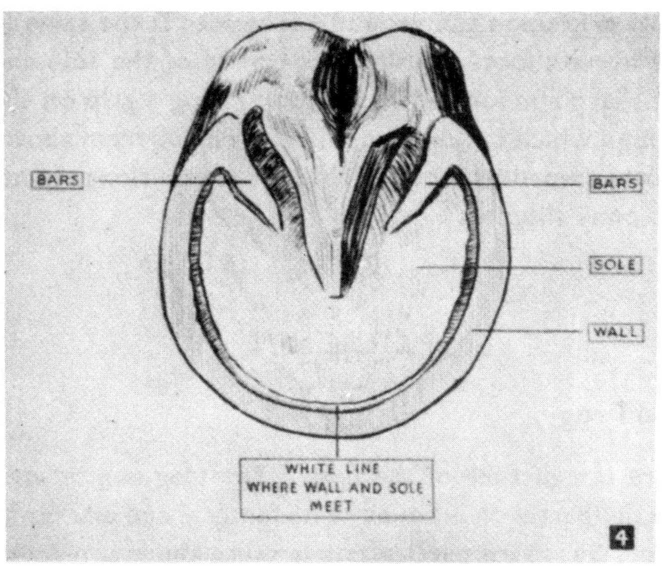

The Sole

Now we come to the sole. The sole covers the ground surface of the foot and its object is to protect the foot from injury from below. Unfortunately it is none too thick for this purpose, but we must remember that nature did not visualise a state of affairs in which nails and pieces of glass are left lying about and so did not make provision against accidents from such causes. The lesson to be learnt here is that any thinning of the sole by the blacksmith when a pony goes to the forge is to be deprecated. Thinning of the sole with his knife makes it look smooth and neat but is a bad practice.

The place where sole meets wall is called the *white line* as indicated in the picture.

There is one interesting point about the sole which is well shown in the next picture.

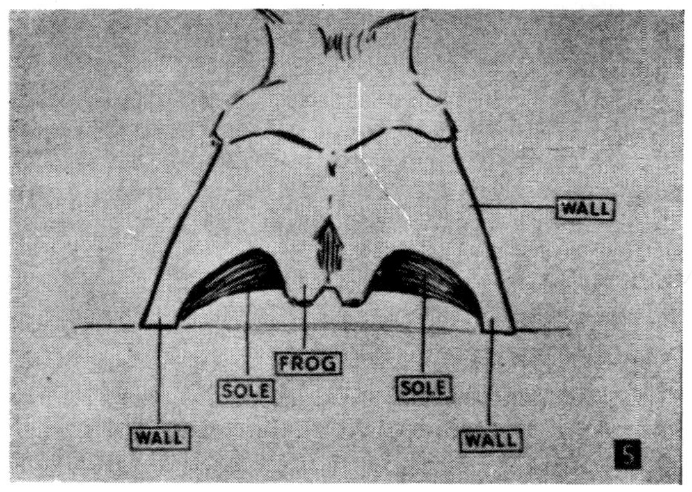

PICTURE No. 5

In the healthy state the sole curves slightly instead of being absolutely flat. The proper way to express this is to say that it is slightly concave. Now you know that if you turn a saucer upside down and press it into the ground it is almost impossible to move it. The concavity of the saucer and its sharp rim give a great grip upon the ground. The idea is the same in the horse's foot, the slight concavity of the sole and the sharp rim formed by the wall giving a grip on the ground which can only be shifted by a pull from above. In other words it is one of nature's precautions against the pony slipping.

The Frog

Here is a picture of the frog.   The frog is a bit of a puzzle, partly on account of its funny shape and funny name, but more particularly because there is nothing like it in our own foot.   It is necessary therefore to explain why nature has given the horse a frog and for what purpose.   Actually the frog is quite one of the most interesting parts of the whole pony's body and shows nature in her most ingenious mood.   In thinking of the frog you must regard it as an anti-slipping and anti-concussion device which in effect is its real purpose.

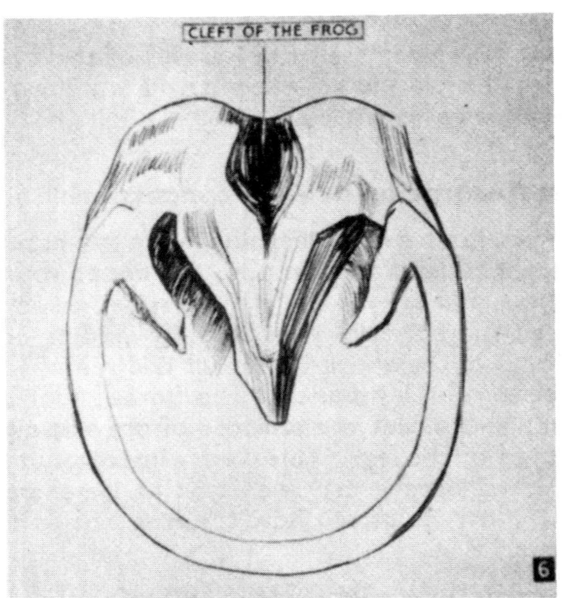

You will appreciate that when a pony needs to pull up sharp or turn, there is considerable risk of him slipping or straining himself unless he can obtain a secure grip on the ground. Likewise, when a pony gallops fast there must be considerable jar to the body at every step, leading eventually to lameness unless some means existed of deadening or absorbing the shock. The frog serves both purposes, anti-slipping and anti-concussion. Let us see how it works.

Anti-slipping

The frog acts as an anti-slipping device in the following ways. First of all, it is made of horn but of a softer kind of horn than the wall or sole. Indeed it is very much like a piece of india-rubber, and just as rubber soles to a pair of shoes give you a grip on the ground—so with the horse's frog. This power is enhanced by the fact that when a horse puts his foot to the ground the frog region is the first part to make contact with the ground. In a fast turn he sticks his feet out thereby lowering the frog even more. Here is one of Major John Board's delightful pictures showing how a polo pony in pulling up short, thrusts his feet forward to press his frogs hard into the ground.

Secondly, the peculiar shape of the frog, pointed towards the front and broad at the back, serves the purpose of driving a wedge, point foremost, into the ground thereby materially assisting in braking power. There can be no other possible explanation for the peculiar shape of the frog.

Lastly, there are the grooves in the frog, namely, the central cleft and those at the sides. Just as the grooves in the cover of a new motor tire act as a precaution against skidding, so do these grooves in the frog help in preventing slipping.

If you have ever seen the imprint of the frog on a dusty road or in muddy ground, you will have an excellent idea of how it works.

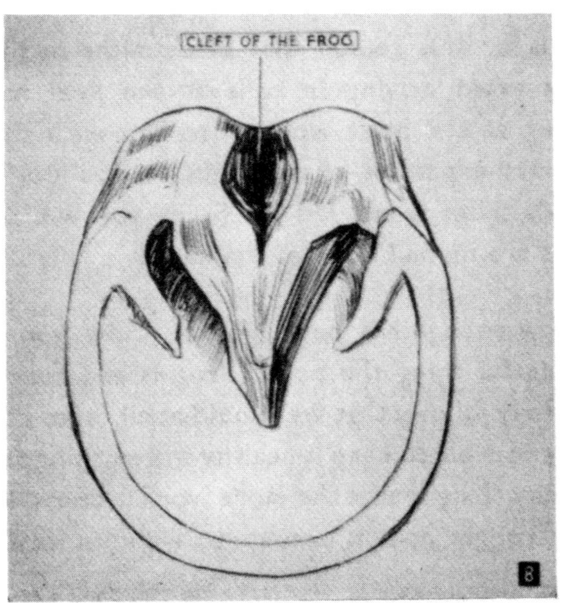

Shock Absorption or Anti-concussion

When you jump over something in the gymnasium you are taught to land on your toes and not on your heels, for if you land on your heels you suffer a very nasty jar to all the bones of your leg. By landing on your toes some of the shock of impact is dispersed before it reaches your leg bones. The horse's frog acts in this way and serves the purpose of preventing jar to the bones of the leg. This is very important for constant jar to the leg may well lead to lameness eventually. Now let us see how the frog acts as a shock absorber.

PICTURE No. 9

When the foot makes contact with the ground the frog yields slightly so absorbing some of the jar. What remains is then transmitted upwards to a soft cushion which lies within the foot just above the frog as shown in the picture. This too yields but in an outward direction, so forcing the heels apart. In other words the jar of impact is transmitted upwards and then dispersed outwards as shown in the dotted line in the picture, thus saving a great deal of concussion from travelling up the bones of the leg.

It is for this reason that blacksmiths in shoeing a pony avoid driving in nails at the heel region, as nailing at the heels would interfere with the slight outward expansion of the heels. If you look at your pony's shoes when you get home you will find that there are no nail holes at the heels.

Now enough has been said to show you what a wonderful thing the pony's frog is and from this it naturally follows that we should at all times do everything possible to keep it healthy and working properly. A funny thing is that the more work it does the larger and stronger does it become, so we must ensure that in shoeing a pony due provision is made for the frog always to come in contact with the ground and so function properly.

So much then for this outline of the structure of the pony's foot.

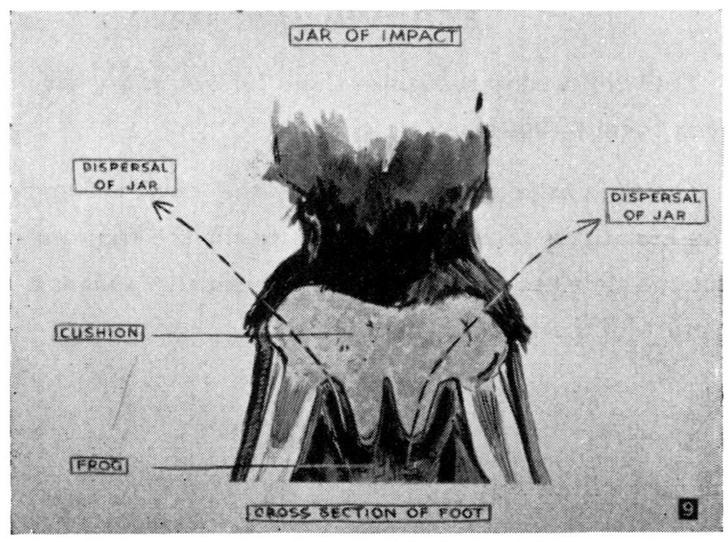

Part Two

SHOEING

The need to shoe a pony—that is to say to fit a band of iron or steel to the foot—is the direct consequence of domestication in that the wear occasioned to the wall on a hard road surface is greater than the rate of new growth sent down from above.

If we persist in working a pony unshod on a hard road the day will eventually arrive when, as a result of extensive wear to wall and sole, the pony goes foot-sore or even lame.   The answer to the problem lies in protecting the foot against such excessive wear by shoeing the pony.

The Romans were our first great road builders and the ponies of the Roman legions in Britain were un-doubtedly shod. Indeed Roman horse shoes are occasionally dug up.   Here is a picture of two Roman horse shoes supplied by courtesy of the London Museum.

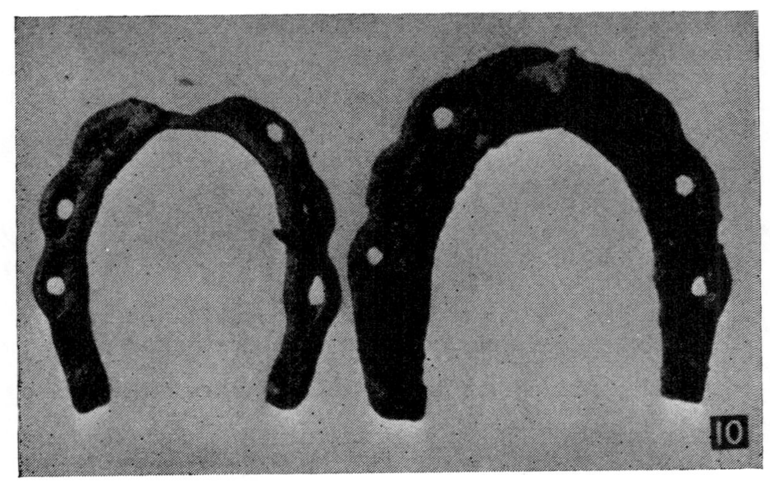

PICTURE No. 10

The easiest way in which to understand shoeing is for us all to pay a supposed visit to a forge and see step by step what goes on there and the reason for each step. So let us now pretend that we are at the forge.

The process of shoeing a pony falls into six definite phases, each of which will be considered in turn.

Phase I

This is called REMOVAL and consists in the removal of
the old shoe.   For this task the blacksmith needs his
'buffer,' 'shoeing hammer' and 'pincers.'   Here is a picture of them.

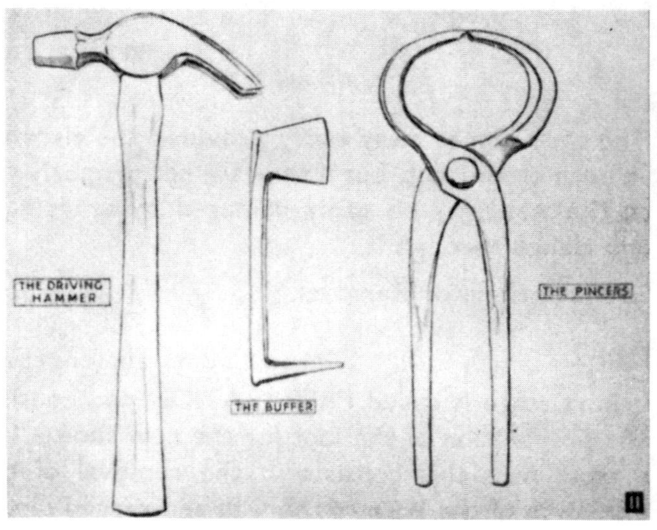

PICTURE No. 11

You will readily recognise them for you must have
seen them in use many times.

The shoe, as you know, is held by the 'clenches.' The first thing to do therefore is to lift the foot and cut the clenches so as to release the shoe.   Here is a picture of the blacksmith doing this.

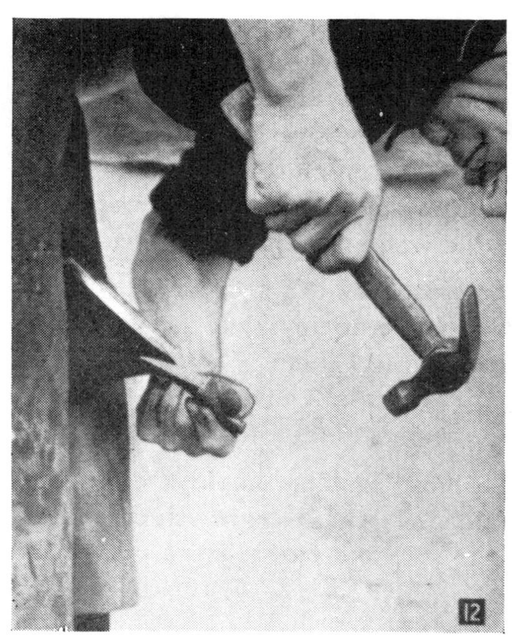

The clenches are cut off clean with the 'buffer,' after which the blacksmith levers off the shoe with his pincers as shown in the next picture.

The shoe comes away easily provided the clenches have been cleanly cut, but if they are not properly cut then the wall may be badly damaged by dragging a rough clench through it.

So much then for removal.

Phase 2

The next stage is called PREPARATION and consists in the preparation of the foot for the new shoe. For the most part this consists in the removal of the overgrowth of the horn of the wall and ragged pieces of the sole and frog. The wall has continued to grow since the pony last went to the forge but has been protected from any wear by the presence of the shoe. Hence it has become overlong making things uncomfortable for the pony, interfering with his action and possibly causing him to stumble. Preparation means reducing the wall once again to its natural length.

PICTURE No. 14

The tools used by the blacksmith at this stage are the drawing knife, toeing knife, hoof cutters and rasp. Here is a picture of them.

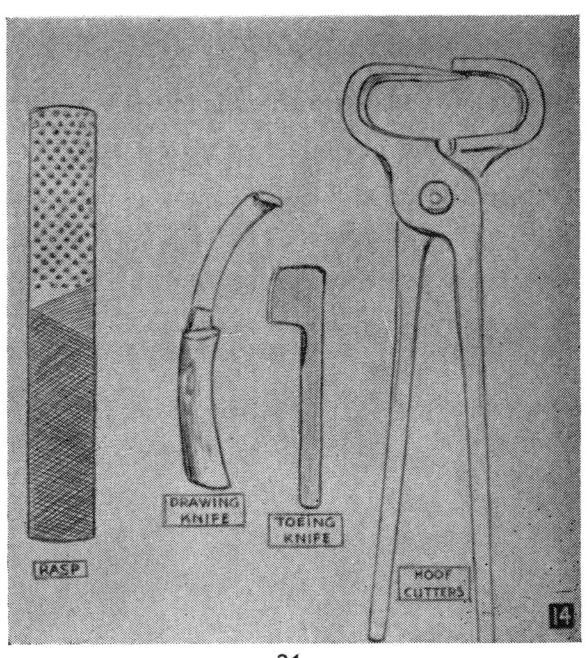

For the most part the blacksmith employs his 'drawing knife' both to cut away the overgrowth of wall and also to tidy up the sole and frog. Here is a picture of him doing this.

The use of this knife on the sole or frog calls for discretion since for reasons already explained the less they are cut about the better.

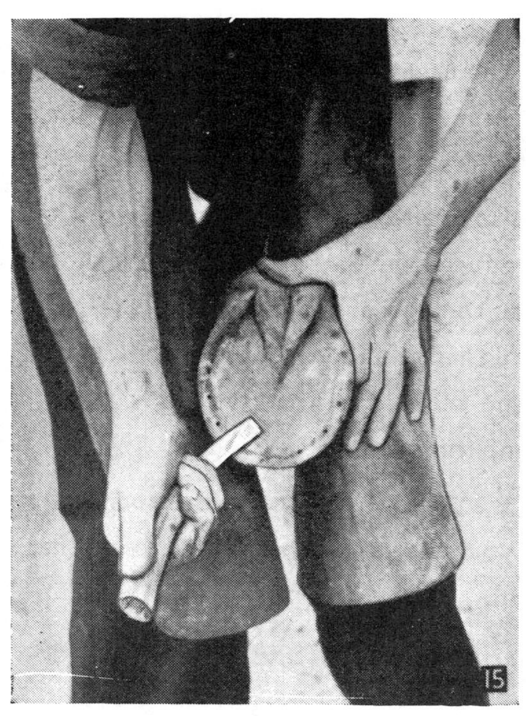

Whatever the blacksmith does in the way of cutting and tidying up he always ends up by using his 'rasp.' Here is a picture of the rasp in action. You will note that he is using it only on the ground surface of the foot.

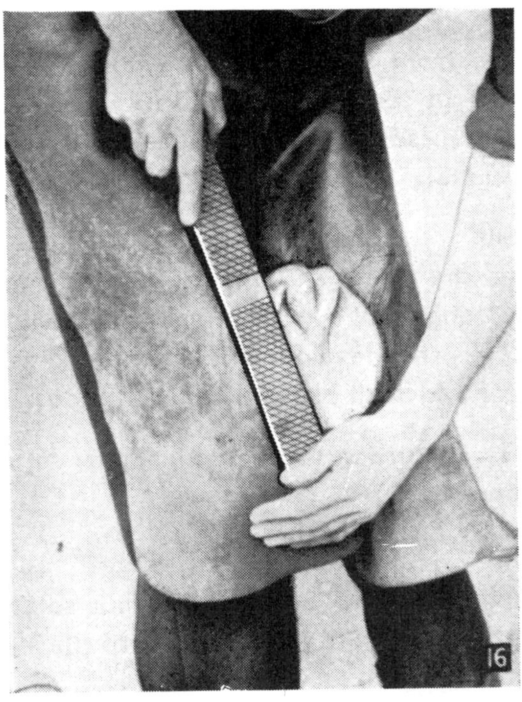

Upon the use of this tool depends the creation of an absolutely level surface to the foot on which the new shoe is to rest.

The blacksmith then inspects his work to see that he has reduced the foot sufficiently, by shortening the length at the toe and by lowering the height at the heels, and that such has been effected equally on both inside and outside so that the pony stands squarely and evenly on his feet.

PICTURE No. 17

Here is a picture of a foot before and after reduction so that you may properly appreciate all that has just been said.

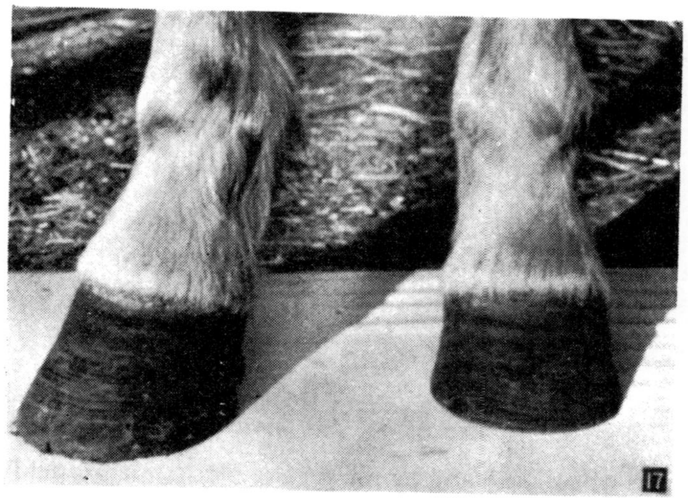

Phase 3

The next stage is called FORGING. This is concerned with the making or forging of the new shoe. For this a fire and anvil are necessary.

The iron from which shoes are made is sold to blacksmiths in long lengths of various weight and shape. The first thing to do therefore is to cut off lengths suitable for the making of the new set of shoes.

For this the use of the mighty 'sledge hammer' is necessary, the tool which more than any other accounts for the development of those grand arm muscles for which all blacksmiths are famous.

Here is a picture of the sledge hammer in use, for
this purpose.

PICTURE No. 18

The iron must now be made red hot so that the
blacksmith can 'turn' it and shape it into the form of a
horse shoe.

So into the fire it goes, held in his fire tongs. Now the fire roars and glows and the sparks fly.

Out it comes and on to the anvil where under the blows of his 'turning hammer' the blacksmith quickly turns and shapes it and makes more sparks fly.

Now for the nail holes fashioned so carefully with the 'stamp' and 'pritchel' and the 'drawing' of the clip. Then the shoe is ready to try on.

Phase 4

The next stage is called FITTING.

The shoe while still slightly hot is carried on a pritchel to the pony's foot and tried on.

Here is a picture showing this.

PICTURE No. 20

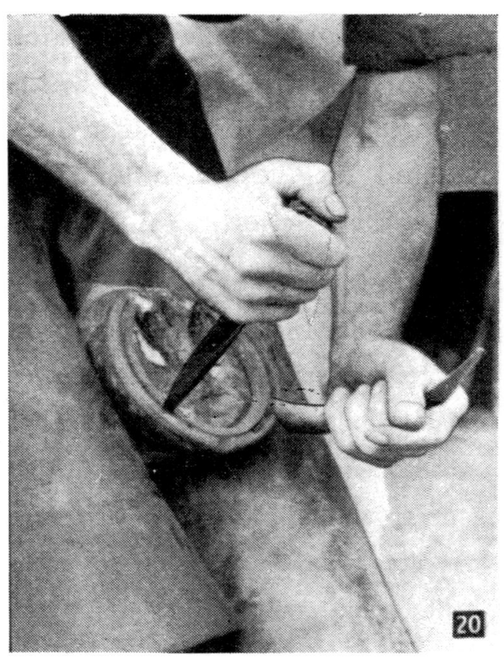

The shoe may prove to be too broad or too narrow and if so adjustments must be made. It will almost certainly be too long at the heels but this is deliberate as the blacksmith likes to cut off the heels, using a tool called a heel cutter, so as to leave them at the exact length required.

The part of the foot on which the new shoe is to rest is called the 'bearing surface,' and if this is not quite level then the horn will be seared by the hot shoe more at one point than another. Here again the necessary adjustments can now be made with the rasp.

The procedure just described to you is known as HOT SHOEING but you will of course appreciate that a fire and anvil are not always available. In such a case the blacksmith is under necessity to resort to the procedure known as COLD SHOEING where a readymade shoe is taken into use, fitted cold and adjusted as far as may be possible in a cold state. Hot shoeing, needless to say, is by far the more satisfactory method. You should always make an effort to take your pony to a forge rather than relying upon the easier expedient of asking the blacksmith to visit you.

Phase 5

The shoe is now ready to nail on, which brings us to the next step, namely NAILING . The blacksmith drives one of the toe nails first of all. By so doing he can then swing the shoe round slightly so that the heels come into their exact position. Note how carefully the nails are driven.

The blacksmith starts off by tapping lightly and only when he is quite sure that the nail is so 'pitched' that it will not go too deep and injure the pony, does he drive it hard home. The point of the nail should come out some distance up the wall—not too far up or it may press and hurt—called 'coarse' nailing—not too low down or the grip on the wall will be insecure—called 'fine' nailing.

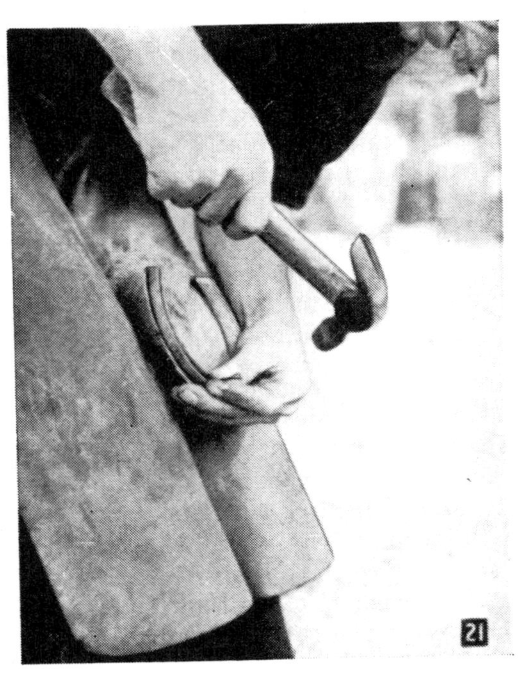

21

The point of each nail where it comes out of the wall is wrenched off with the claw of the hammer, leaving a small piece projecting which eventually forms the clench.

How many nails should a blacksmith use? The answer generally given is seven—three on the inside and four on the outside. A better answer, however, is to say "the minimum necessary for security" and only the blacksmith knows just how many that may be, though often it is seven. When an odd number of nails is used why are more placed on the outside than the inside? The answer here is that the outer side of the hoof takes a slightly longer sweep at the quarters than the inside and also that it is slightly thicker.

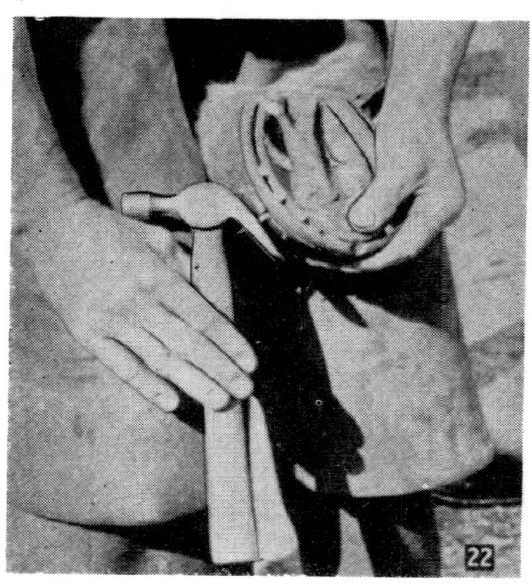

Shoeing nails are made in various sizes to suit different sized horses and ponies, but they are all of this peculiar shape which is quite unlike any other kind of nail you know. Note the bevel on one side of the point. Its object is to direct the point of the nail outwards instead of inwards when being driven, that is to say away from the sensitive parts of the foot. If you watch a blacksmith nailing on a shoe you will see that he always glances at each nail before putting it into the shoe, so as to make sure that it goes in the right way round which means with the bevel to the inside.

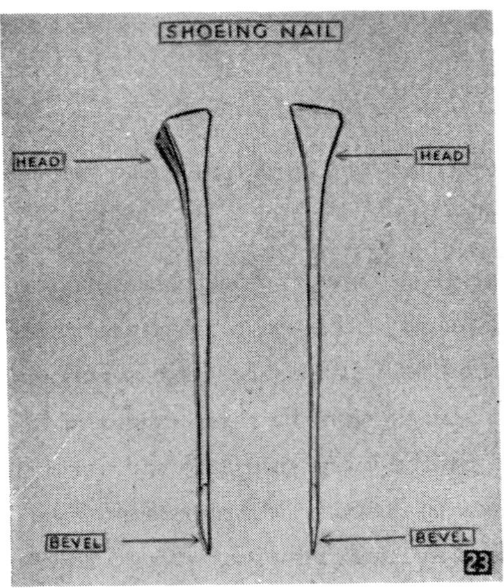

The peculiar shape of the nail head is explained in the next picture.

PICTURE No. 24

This shows a new shoe, a partly wcrn shoe and a badly worn shoe. Note that in each case what remains of the nail head is always larger than the nail hole so that the shoe cannot fall off so long as any head to the nail remains.

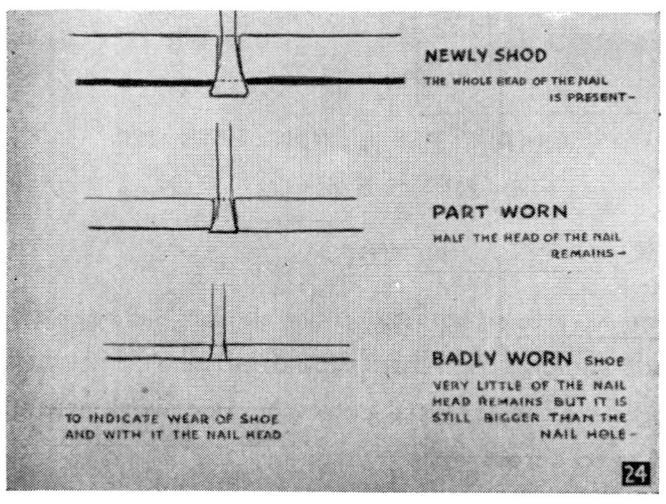

Phase 6

And now for the last step called FINISHING .

PICTURE No. 25

The blacksmith makes the clenches, tightens them up and 'beds' them firmly.

He then gives them a final rub with the rasp to smooth them off.   The toe clip is tapped back lightly into its position.   Lastly the rasp is run round the rim of the wall to blunt its sharp edge and to prevent splitting.   So the job is complete and our visit to the forge comes to an end.   All should now be well for another month when a further visit to the forge will be necessary.

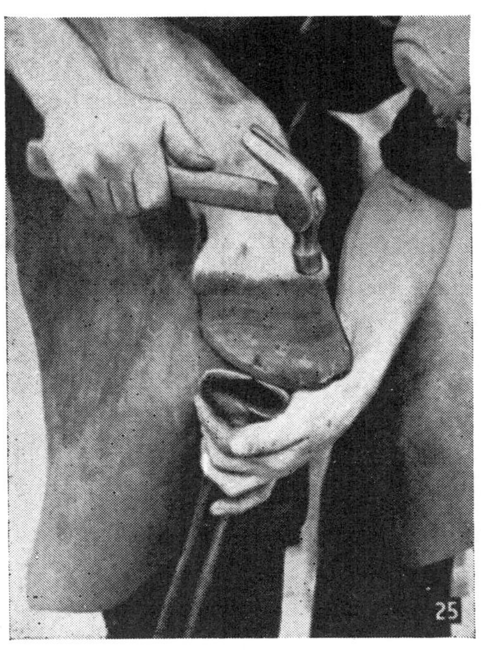

Part Three

WHAT TO LOOK FOR IN THE NEWLY SHOD FOOT

PICTURE No. 26

If you have been able to follow all that has been said about shoeing, then you should be in a position to appreciate the essential points of good workmanship and so to detect what is wrong.

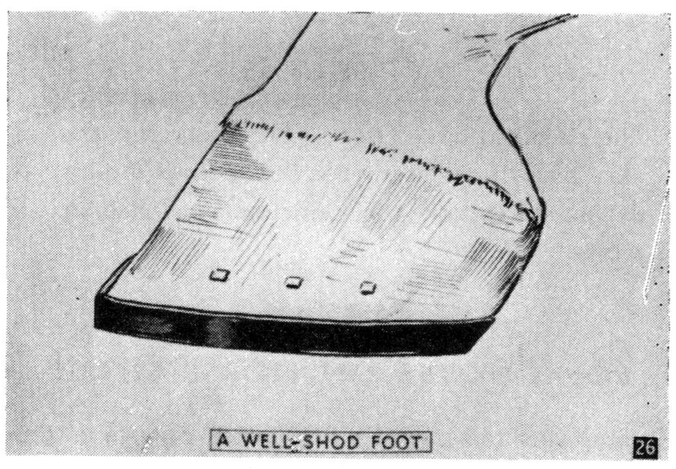

The following are among the more important things to look for in a newly shod foot.

1. First and foremost, the shoe must have been made to fit the foot and not the foot the shoe.

That is to say that there has been no dumping or rasping away of horn to meet shoe. Such is shown by rasp marks over the lower portion of the wall. Sometimes an attempt is made to mask them by smearing the tar brush over the foot.

2. Secondly, the foot must have been reduced in length suitably both at toe and heels and equally so in both the near and off foot, and the frogs must be able to make contact with the ground.

3. Thirdly, the shoe must be of suitable weight for the pony and of a type suitable for the work required of him.

4. There must have been no abuse of the knife on the sole or frog, that is to say that such has been limited to a light trimming only.

5. The heels of the shoe must be the right length, not too long and not too short.

6. The clenches must afford a good hold being placed a sufficient distance up the wall, neatly made and finished off.

7. No daylight should show between iron and horn particularly at the heel region.

8. The clip must be neatly drawn and accommodated.

Part Four

INDICATIONS

THAT RE-SHOEING IS NECESSARY

PICTURE No. 27

The following are among the more obvious signs :

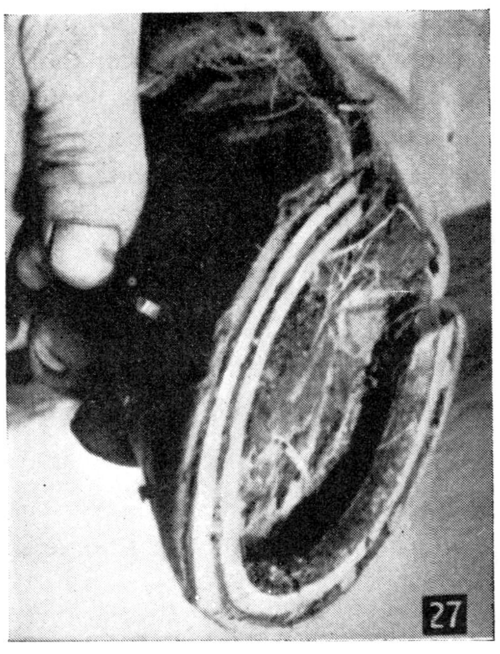

1. The foot has become overlong, overgrown and out of shape so that the shoe no longer fits the foot. This is well shown in the picture.

2. The shoe has worn thin.   In the picture it is seen that the pony has worn the shoe thin mostly on one side.

3. The shoe is loose or has become 'cast', i.e. lost.

PICTURE No. 28

4. The clenches have risen.   The picture is that of a very badly neglected foot but it does indicate the extent to which the clenches may rise in such a case.

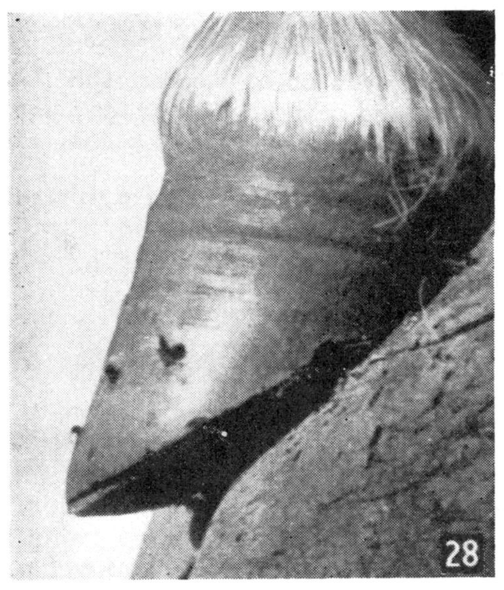

Part Five

SOME NOTES ON HORSE SHOES

We end this talk with a few notes on horse shoes themselves.

Actually this is quite a big subject, for just as in your own case there are shoes and shoes, those suitable for outdoors, for indoors, for the gymnasium, for dancing and so on, similarly with the pony. What is suitable for harness work is not suitable for hunting and what is good on the road is not good on grass. However, in order to limit what is said and not confuse you with too much detail these remarks will be confined to that special type of shoe suitable for a pony engaged in work on grass namely, hunting, gymkhanas and show jumping, which is what mostly concerns you.

The Fore Shoe
To begin with, here is a picture of a horse shoe in its simplest form.

PICTURE No. 29

You will note that it consists of an unmodified bar of iron shaped into a shoe, 'stamped' with nail holes and provided with a single clip. Its name is a 'plain stamped shoe.' Such is suitable only for a pony doing relatively slow work, for the simple reason that it affords little grip on the ground.

Let us now proceed to convert this shoe step by step into the kind of shoe we need for a pony working at a fast pace on grass.

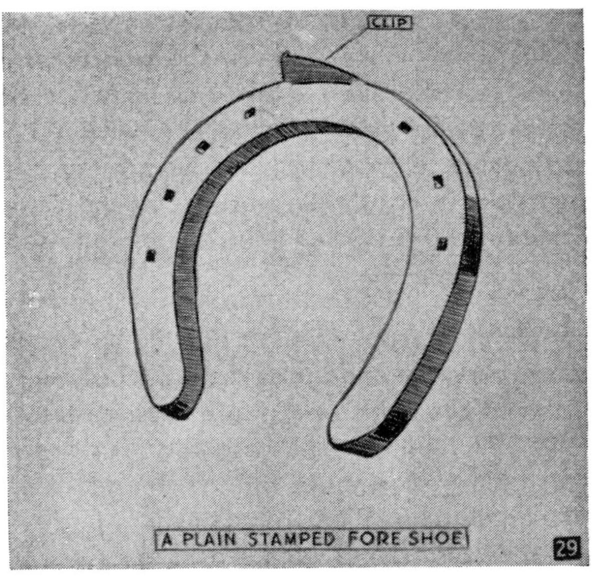

The first modification necessary is to make our shoe of 'concave' iron instead of plain iron. The next picture shows what is meant.

The special feature of concave iron is that it is narrower below than above.   On the left is the shoe made of plain iron.   On the right that made of concave iron.   The idea here is anti-suction, that is to say a precaution against the shoe being sucked off in mud or clay.   Furthermore you will see that the use of concave iron carries on nature's intention that the ground surface of the foot should be concave and the rim should present a sharp edge.   Such a shoe is ideal for work on grass as it bites into the soft ground with little risk of being sucked off.

Our next modification is to 'fuller' the shoe.   Here is a picture of a fullered shoe compared with one that is not fullered.

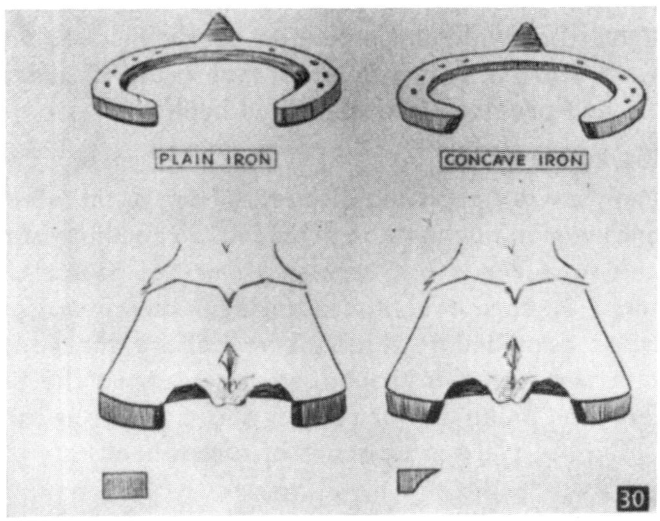

Fullering is a groove made in the iron to give it a roughened surface like the grooves provided on the sole of a pair of golfing shoes and with the same object, namely, a good grip on the ground. When hacking along a road this groove collects little bits of grit and dirt which also helps to prevent slipping.

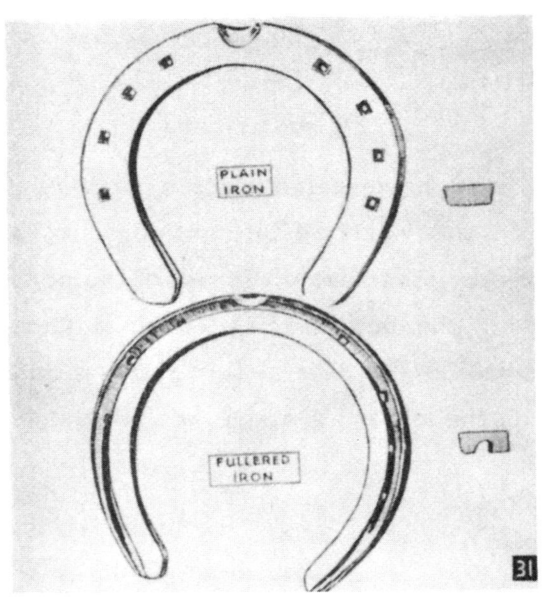

Now for the heels. With a fast moving horse there is always the risk that the toe of the hind foot may make contact with the heels of the fore shoe and tear the shoe off.   To minimise the chance of this happening it is customary to smooth off the heels of the fore shoe—a procedure called 'pencilling.'

For your pony therefore working on grass, a plain stamped shoe is not good.   What the blacksmith ought to provide and indeed in nearly all cases what he does provide, is a fullered shoe made of concave iron and provided with pencilled heels.

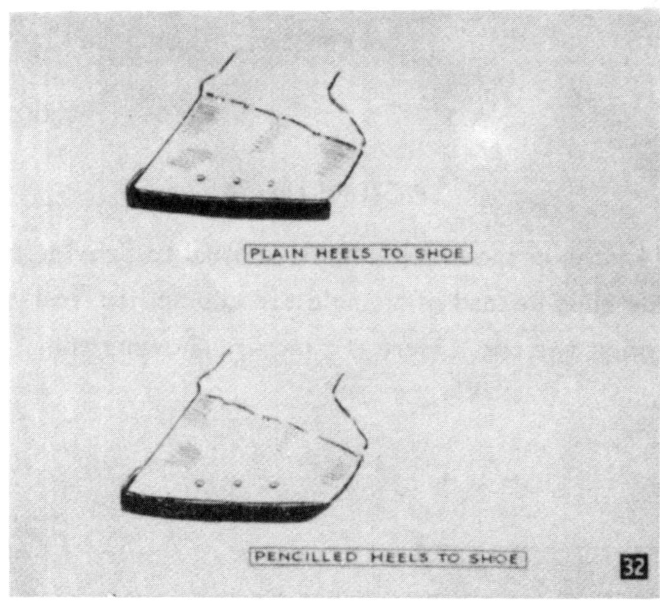

The Hind Shoe

Finally a word about hind shoes.   Here again fullered concave iron ought to be provided.   Pencilling of the heels however is not necessary since of course they cannot be torn off.   Instead a slight downward projection provided at the back will afford the pony a better grip on the ground, so necessary to the hind feet when pulling up or turning short.   Such is called a 'calkin.'   Here is a picture of such a heel.

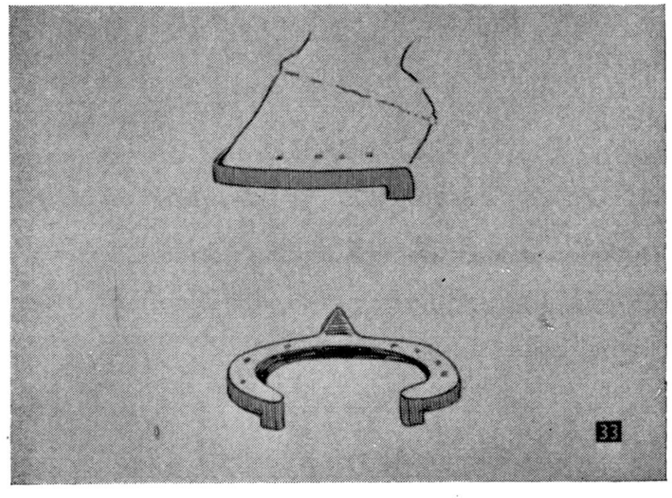

It is usual however to place a modified form of calkin on the inner side, something that is neater and projects less to avoid the risk of the pony hitting or cutting the opposite leg. Such is known as a 'wedge heel.' The next picture shows a shoe with a calkin on the left and a wedge heel on the right.

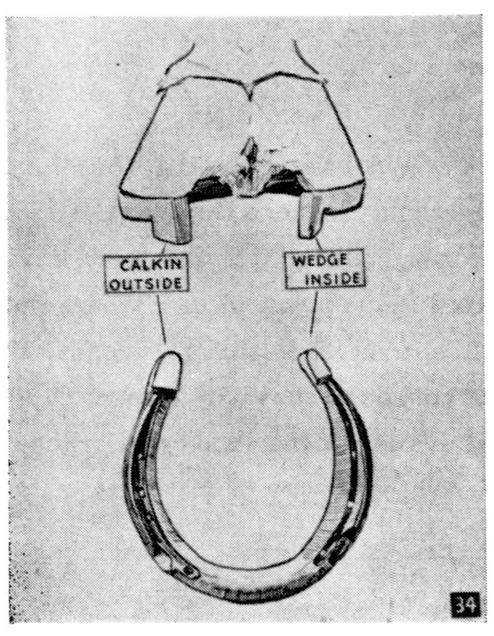

Lastly, in shoeing behind it is usual to provide two side clips instead of a single toe clip and to 'roll' the iron at the toe.   Here is a picture showing this.

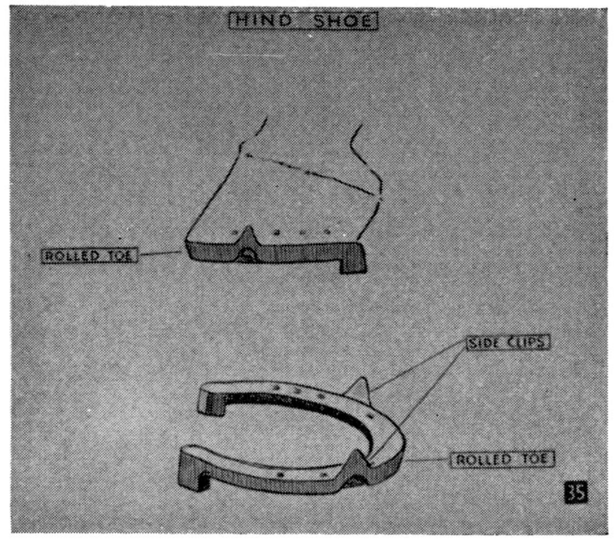

This is a precaution against the accident known as 'over-reaching.' The next picture shows how the accident happens.

You will readily understand that the injury inflicted in the top picture, where the horse is shod behind with a toe clip, is likely to be much more severe than that inflicted in the lower picture where the horse is shod with quarter clips and the iron at the toe is rolled. A rolled toe shoe with quarter clips is a most important feature in the shoeing of galloping ponies, and such ought always to be provided.

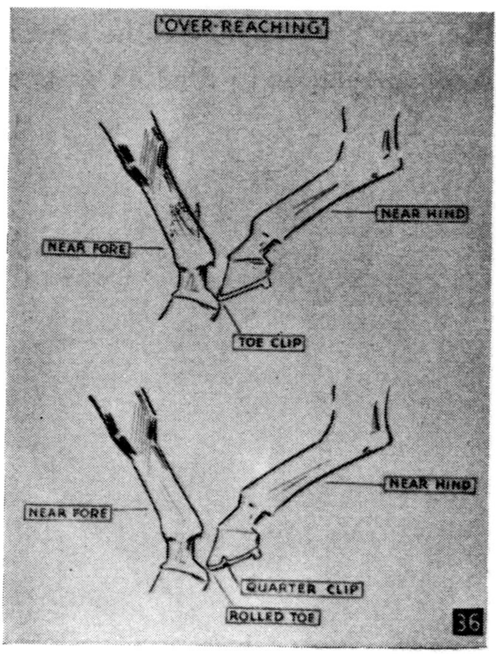

And so the final picture.

PICTURE No. 37

These drawings illustrate the perfect hunter fore and hunter hind shoe such as your pony needs for the kind of work he carries out for you when used on grass at a fast pace.

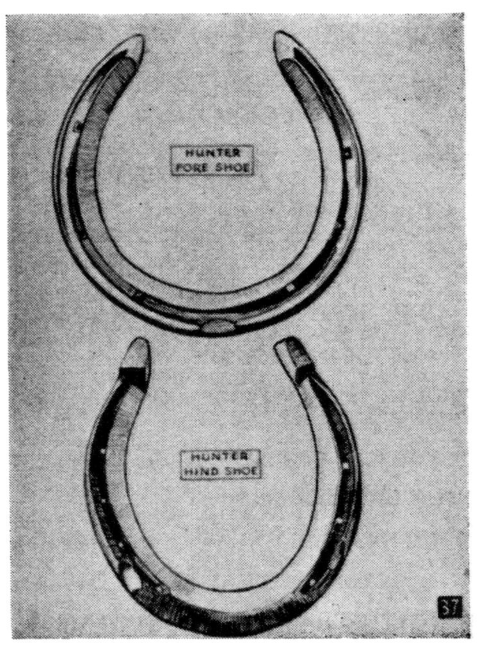

OTHER OFFICIAL PUBLICATIONS

British Horse Society Publications
"RULES FOR DRESSAGE"
"RULES FOR COMBINED TRAINING"
*"RIDING" by Mrs. V. D. S. Williams

Pony Club Publications
*"THE INSTRUCTORS' HANDBOOK"
*"THE MANUAL OF HORSEMANSHIP"
*"TRAINING THE YOUNG HORSE AND PONY"
*"KEEPING A PONY AT GRASS" by Mrs. O. Faudel-Phillips, F.I.H.
*"MOUNTED GAMES AND GYMKHANAS"
"QUIZ QUESTIONS"
*"POLO FOR THE PONY CLUB"
*"A GUIDE TO THE PURCHASE OF CHILDREN'S PONIES"
*"RIDING TO HOUNDS"
"NOTES FOR FIVE-MINUTE LECTURES—FOXHUNTING"
"THE PONY CLUB YEAR BOOK"

*"BASIC TRAINING FOR YOUNG HORSES & PONIES" by
Mrs. V. D. S. Williams
"THE GENERAL PURPOSE SEAT" by Col. The Hon. C. G. Cubitt,
D.S.O., T.D., D.L. and Col. G. T. Hurrell, O.B.E.
*"BITS AND BITTING" by Col. The Hon. C. G. Cubitt
*"THE AIDS AND THEIR APPLICATION" by Col. The Hon. C. G. Cubit
D.S.O., T.D., D.L.
Film Strips are also available for each of these titles

An up-to-date price list of Pony Club publications is shown in the
Pony Club Year Book, issued annually, and is available from Head-
quarters, address as below.

These and other publications connected with the horse are
available from

THE BRITISH HORSE SOCIETY
National Equestrian Centre, Kenilworth
Warwickshire, CV8 2LR

These are available from
BARRON'S
113 Crossways Park Drive
Woodbury, New York 11797